Love In The Mist

Valentine's Day Coloring Book

Your Love Your Way

Just Color It

Anny Will

Happy Coloring

Love is like a cloud

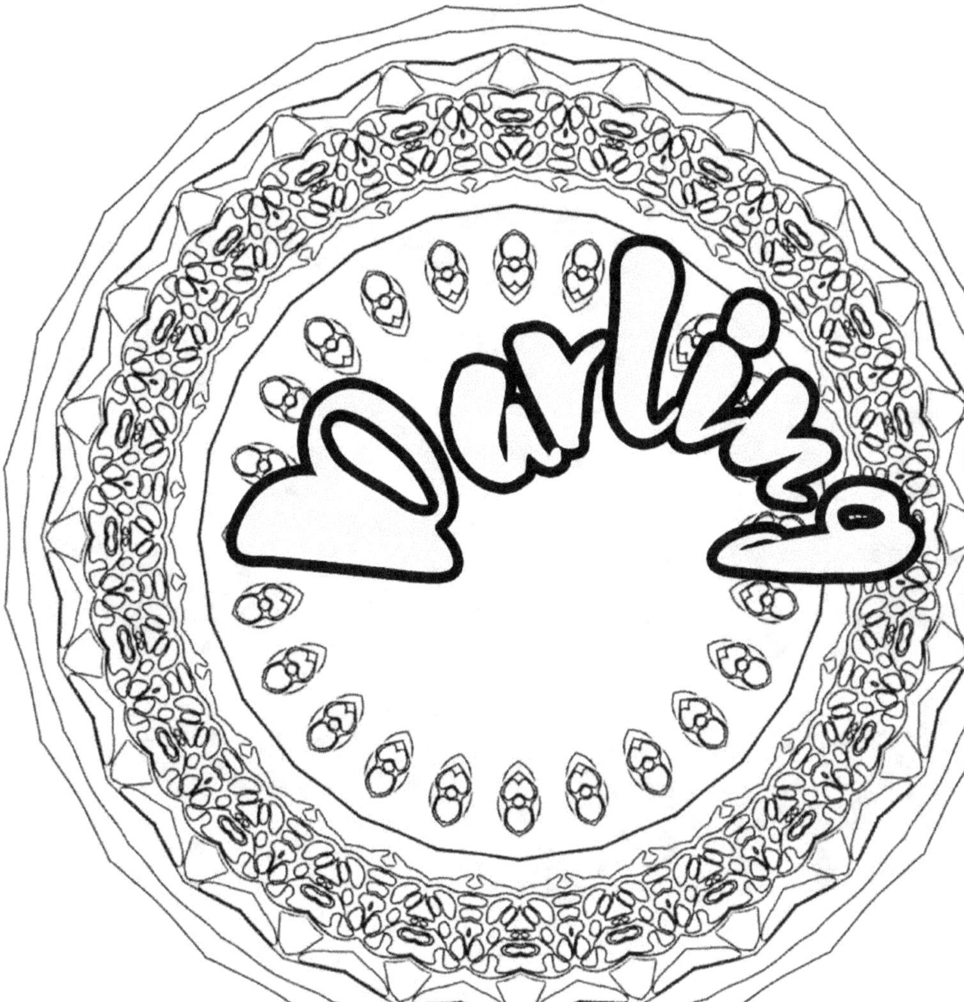
Darling

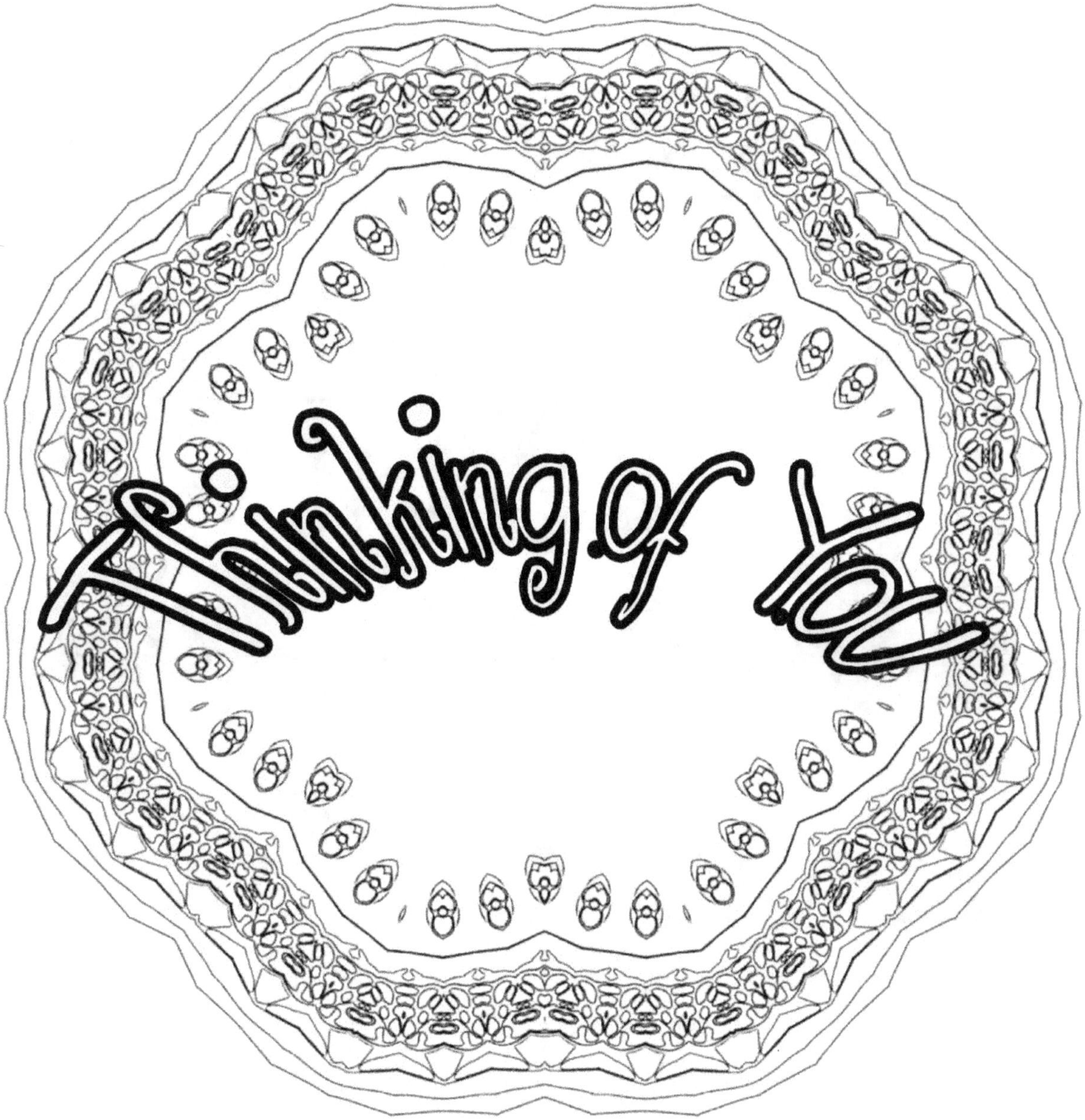
Thinking of You

Dreaming of You

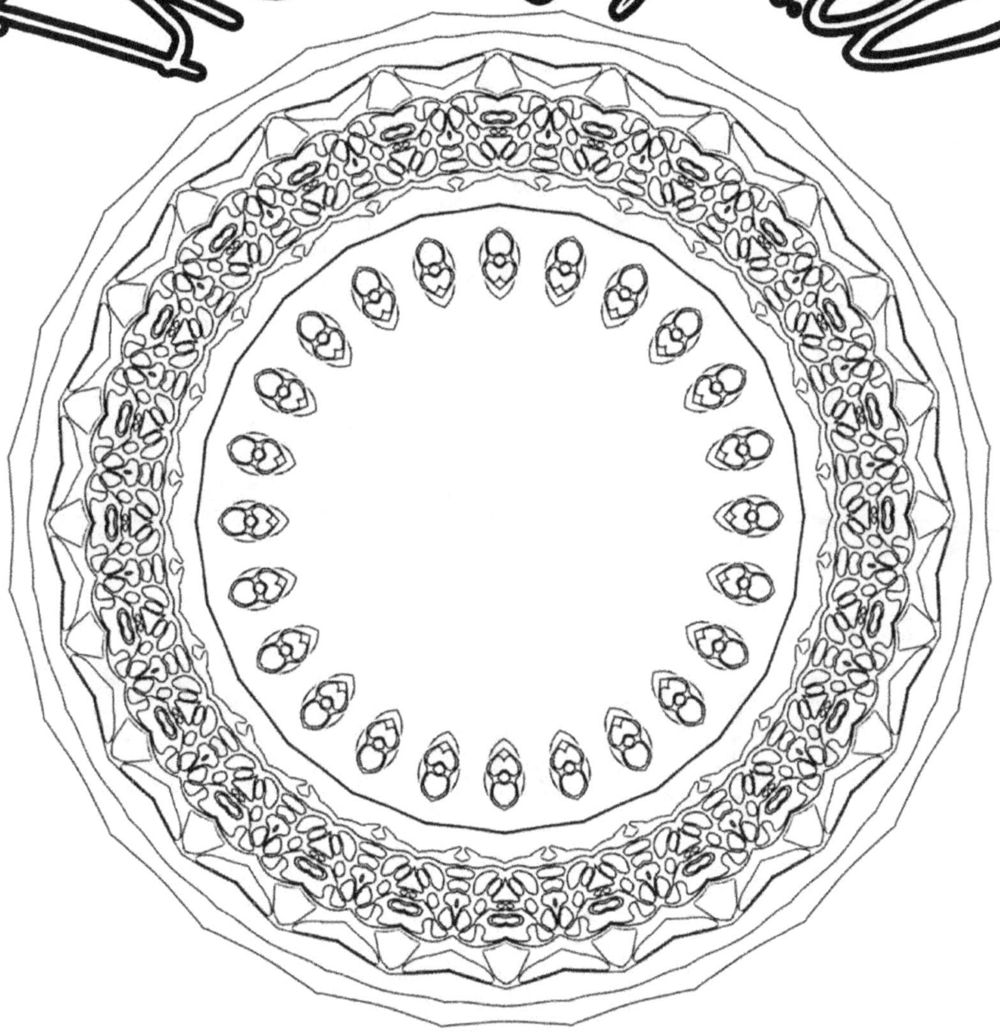

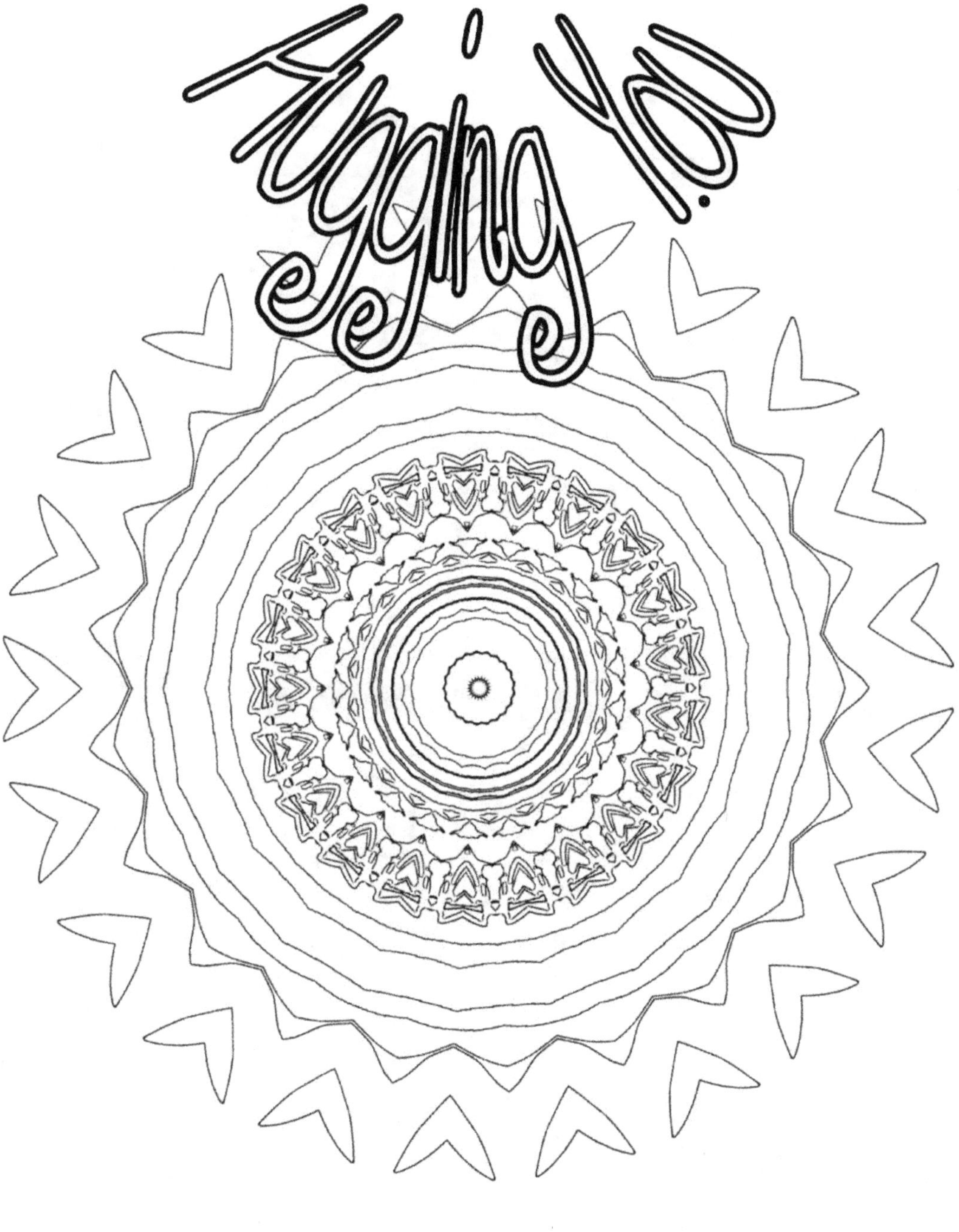
Hugging You

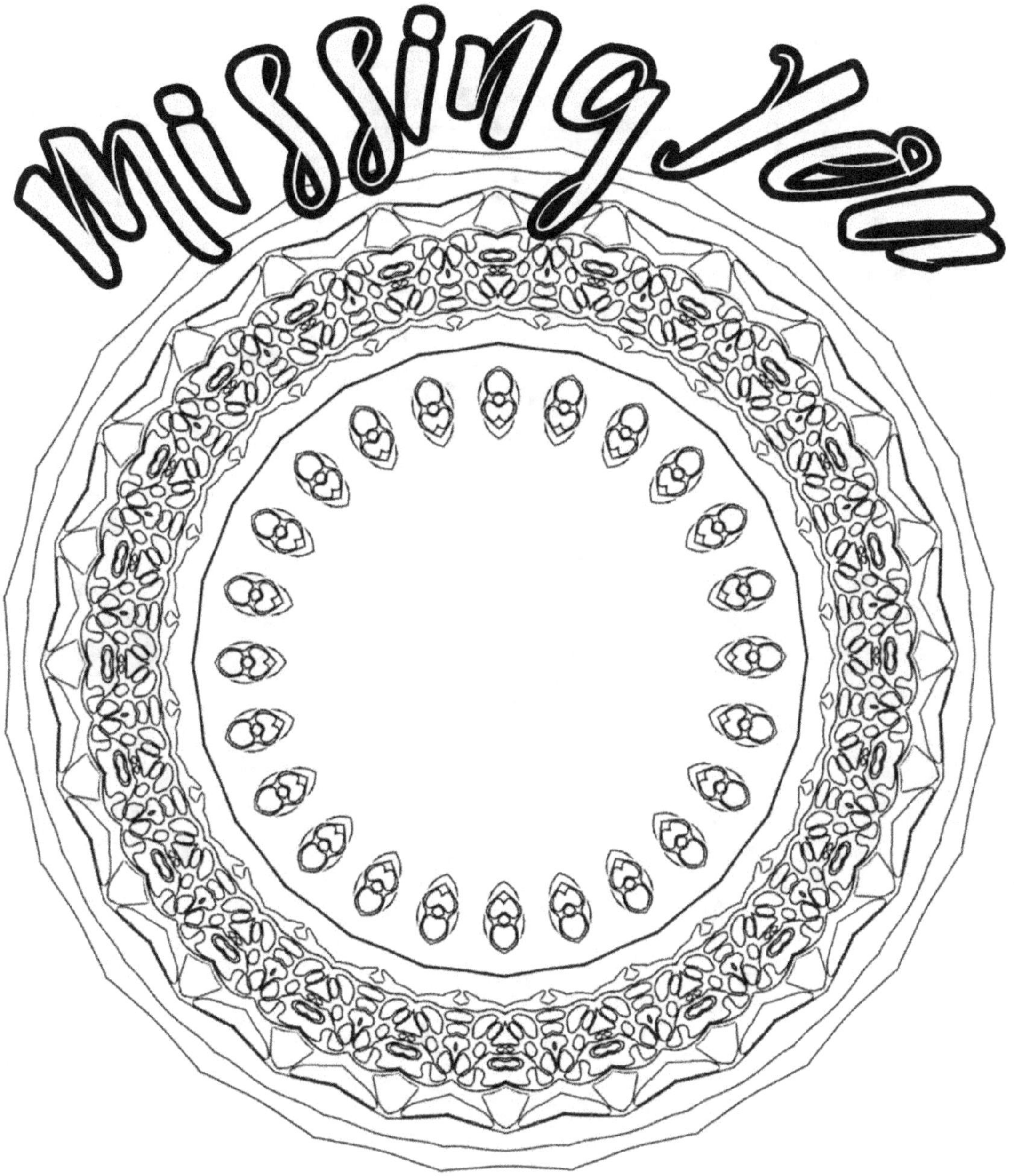
Missing You

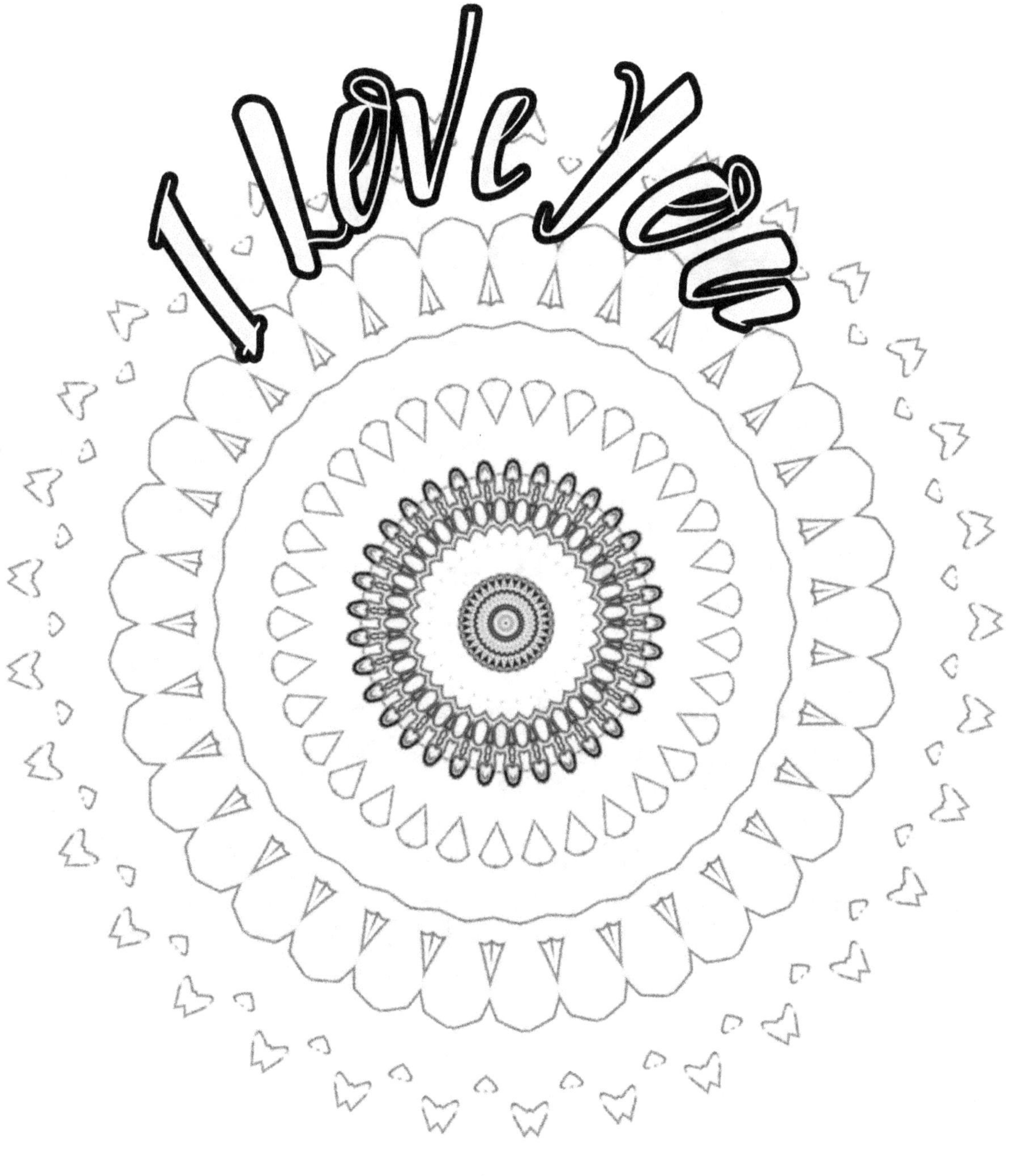
I Love You

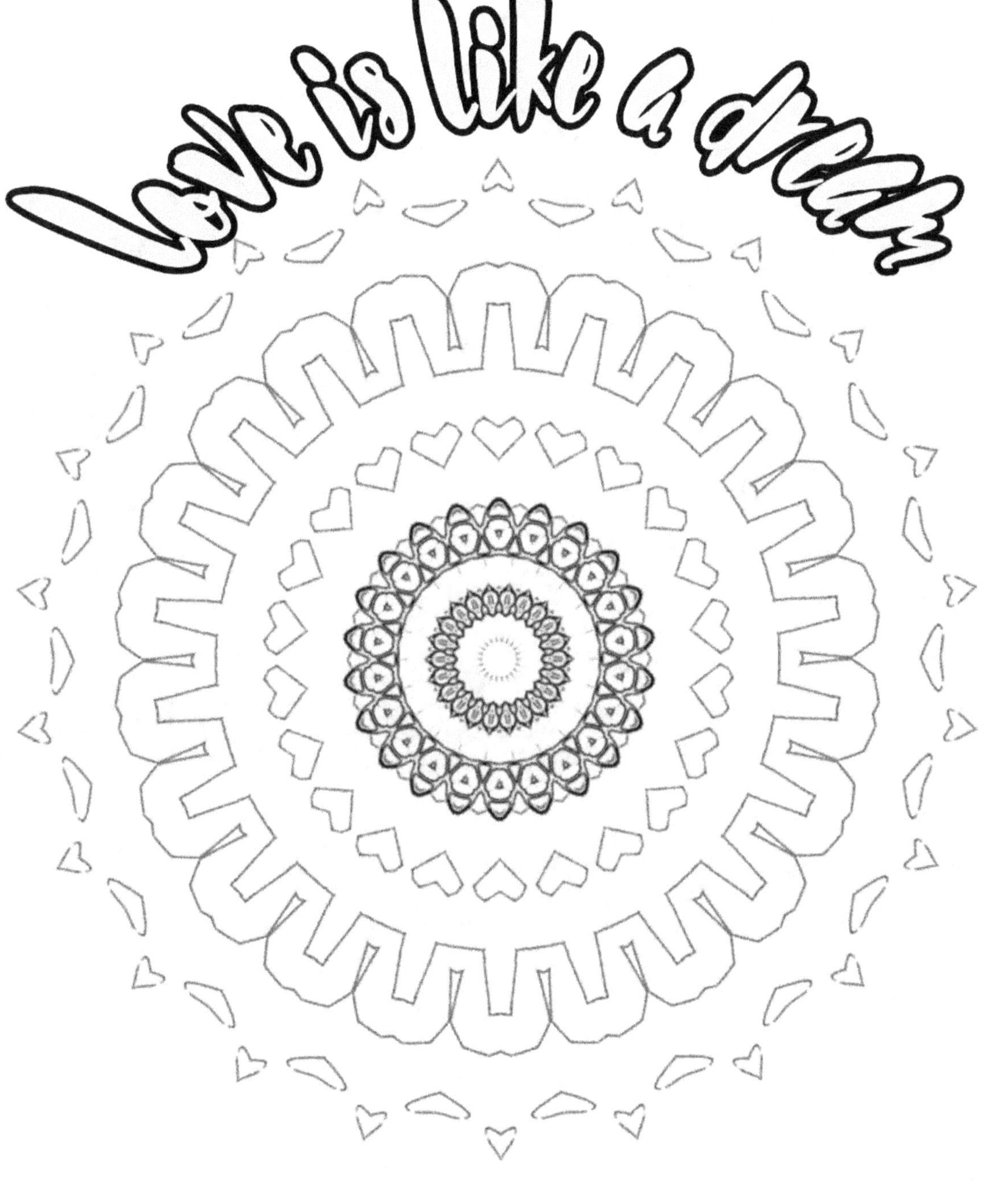
love is like a dream

SWEETHEART

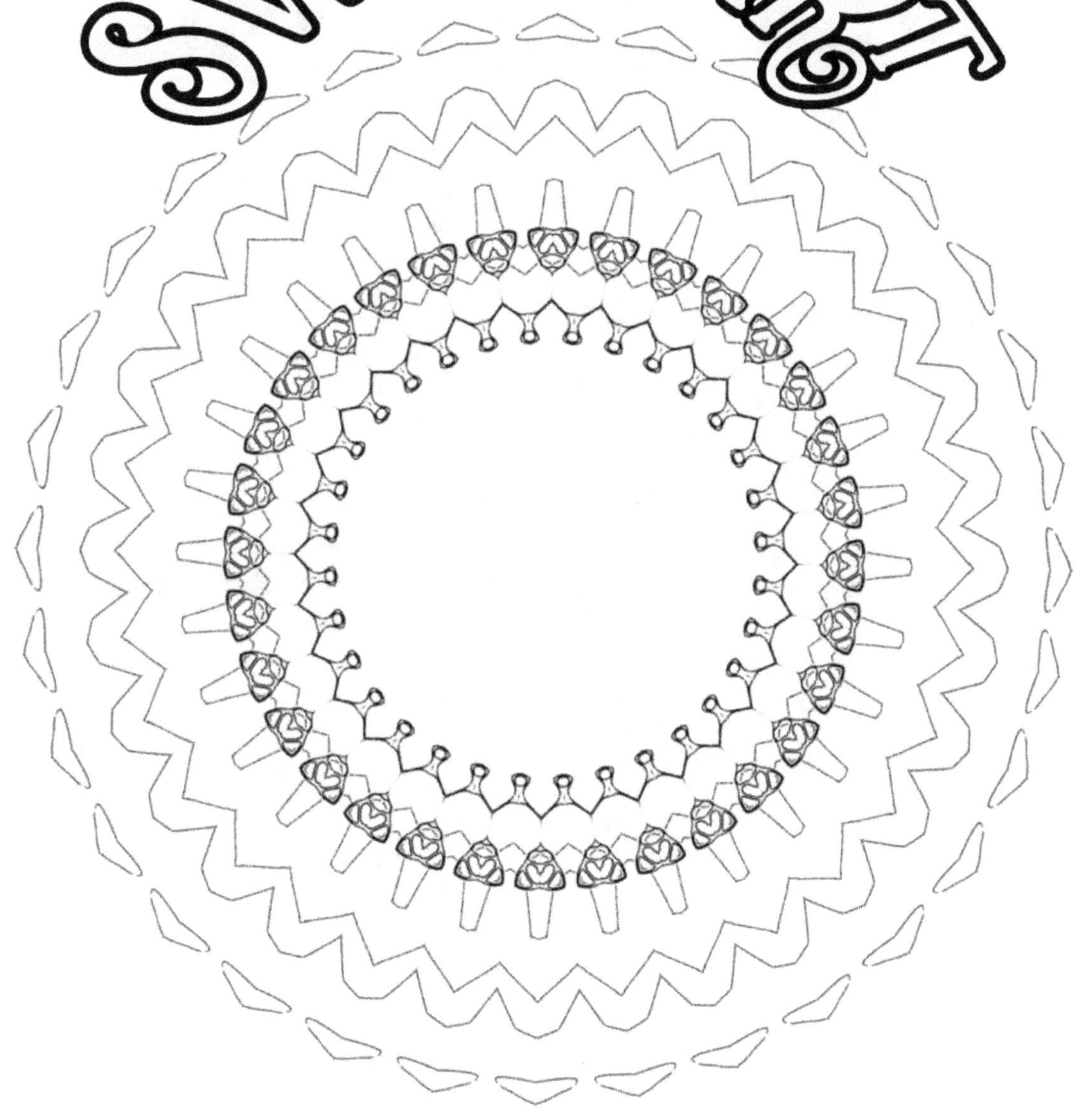

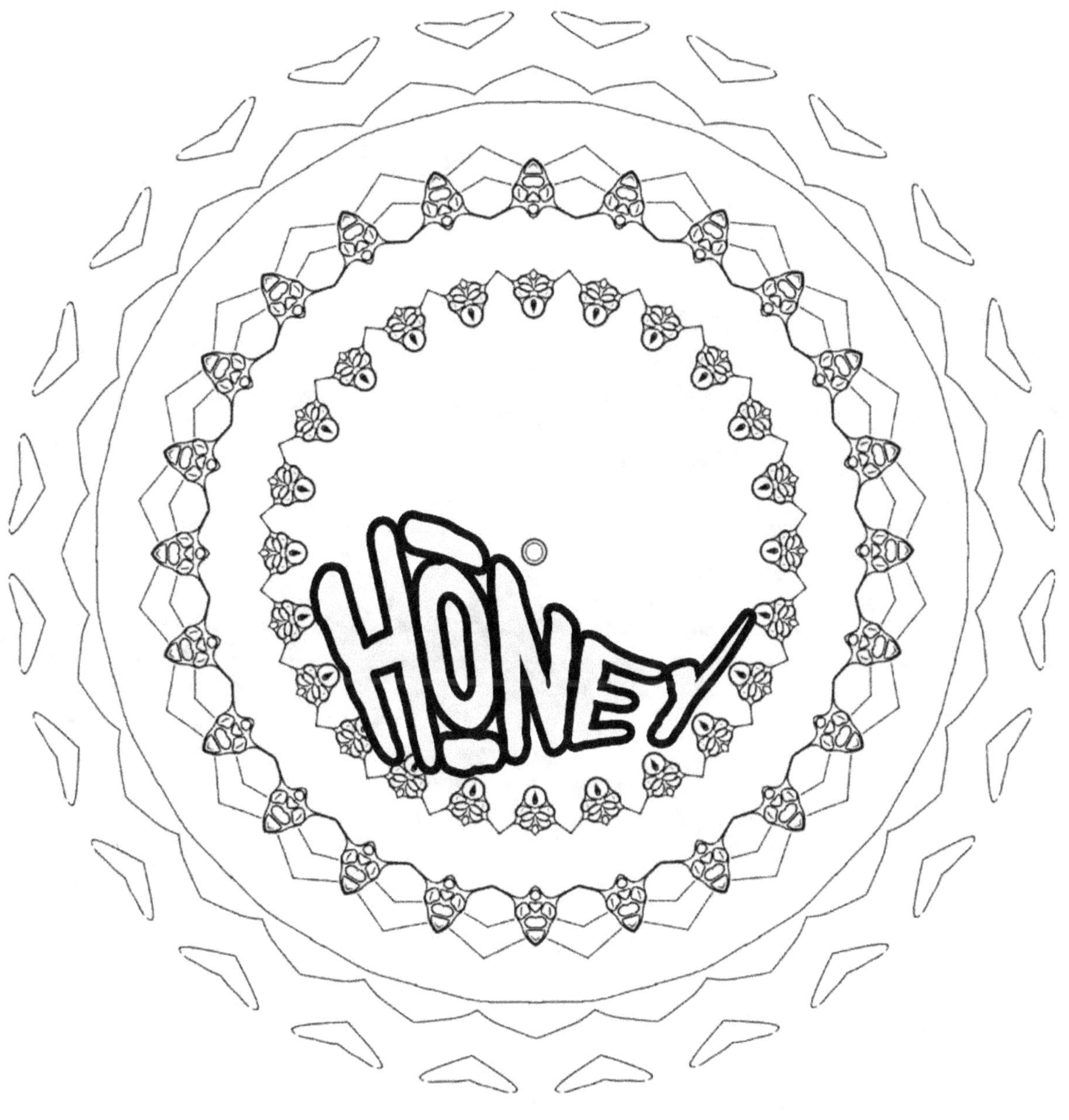
HONEY

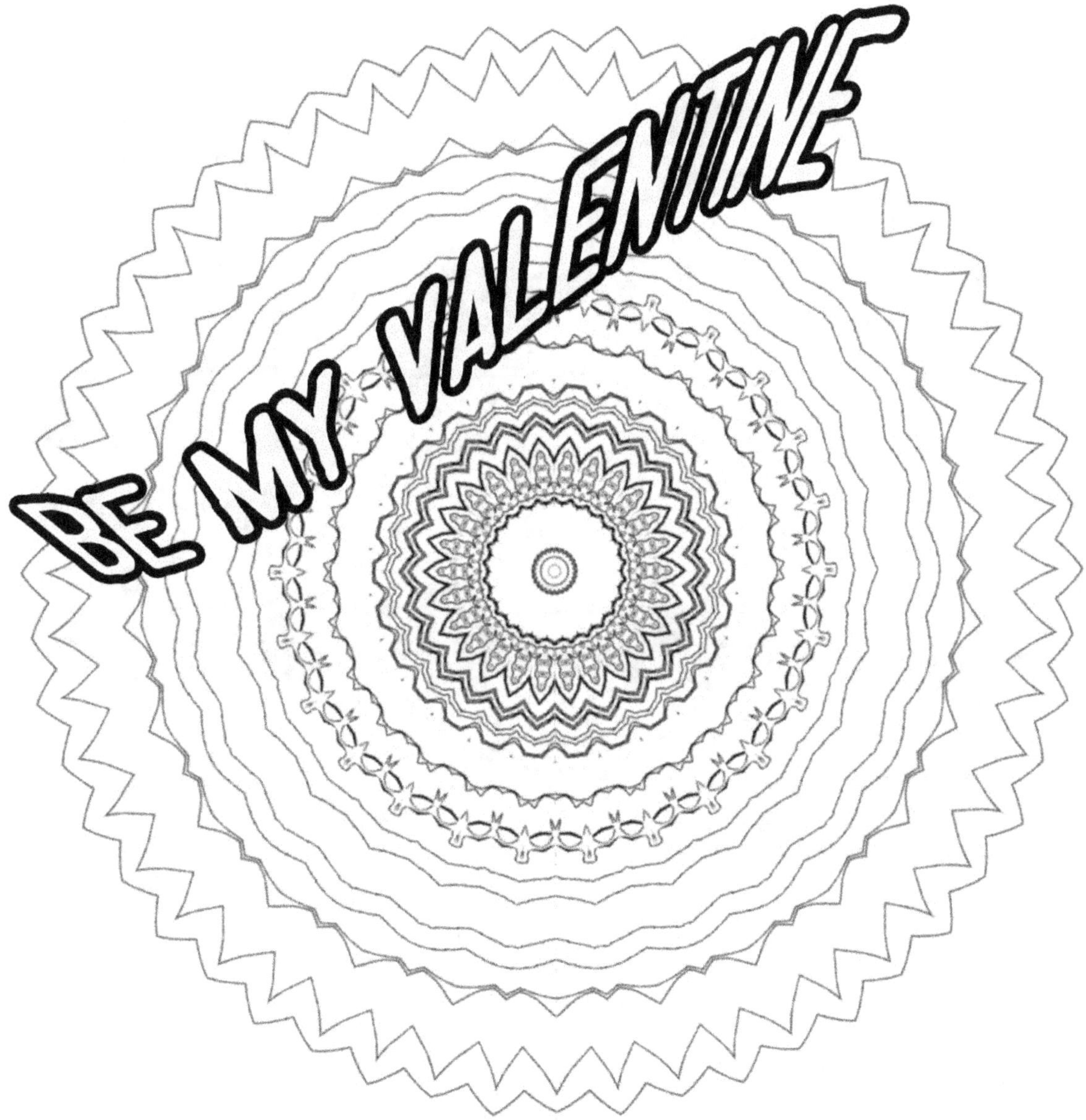
BE MY VALENITINE

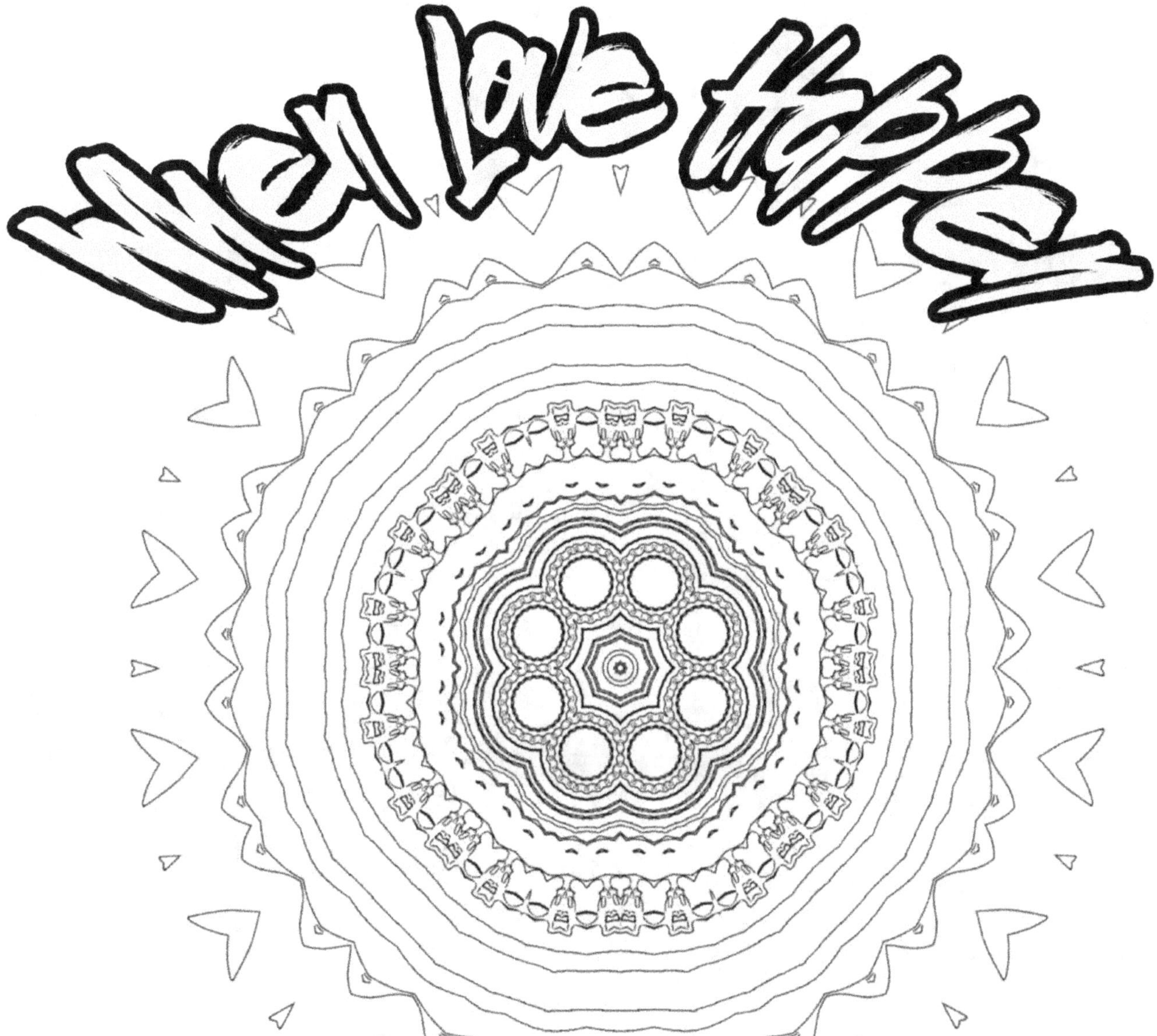
When Love Happen

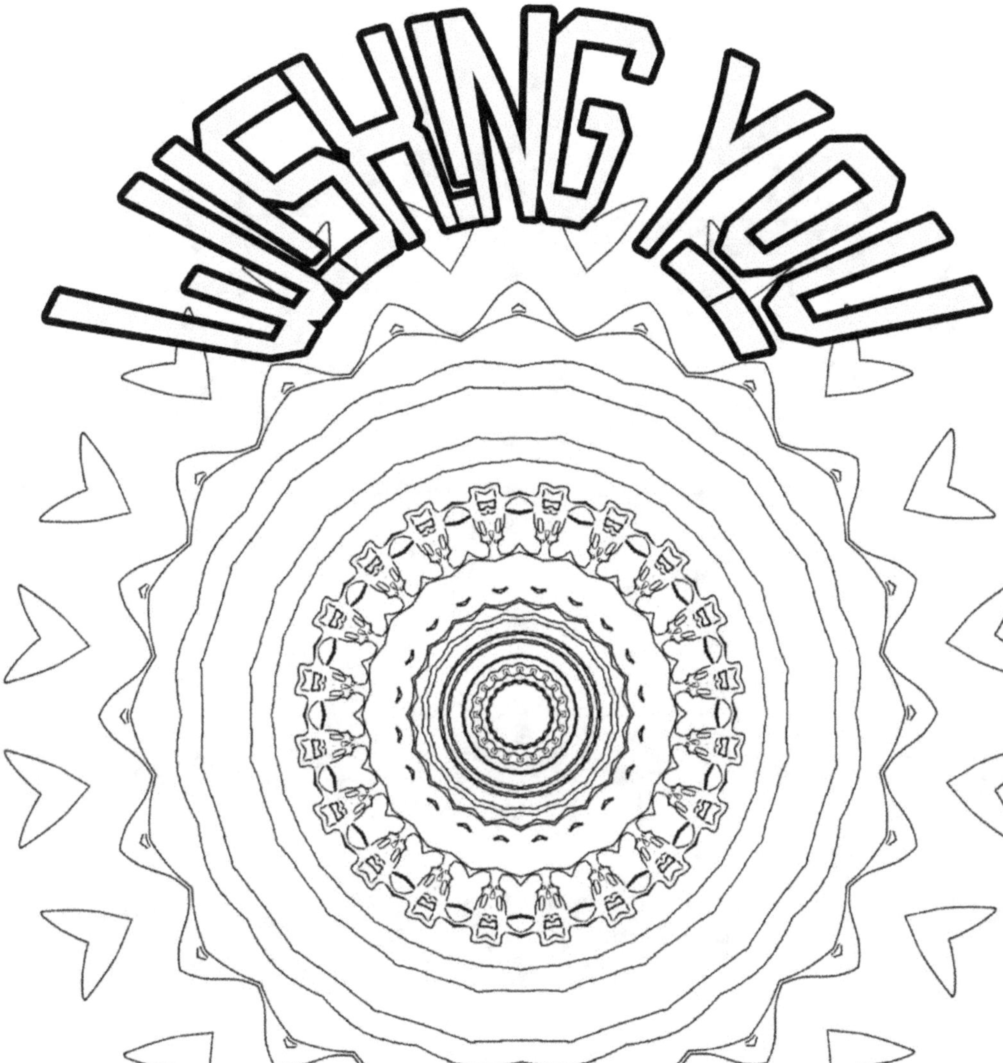
WISHING YOU

I LOVE YOU

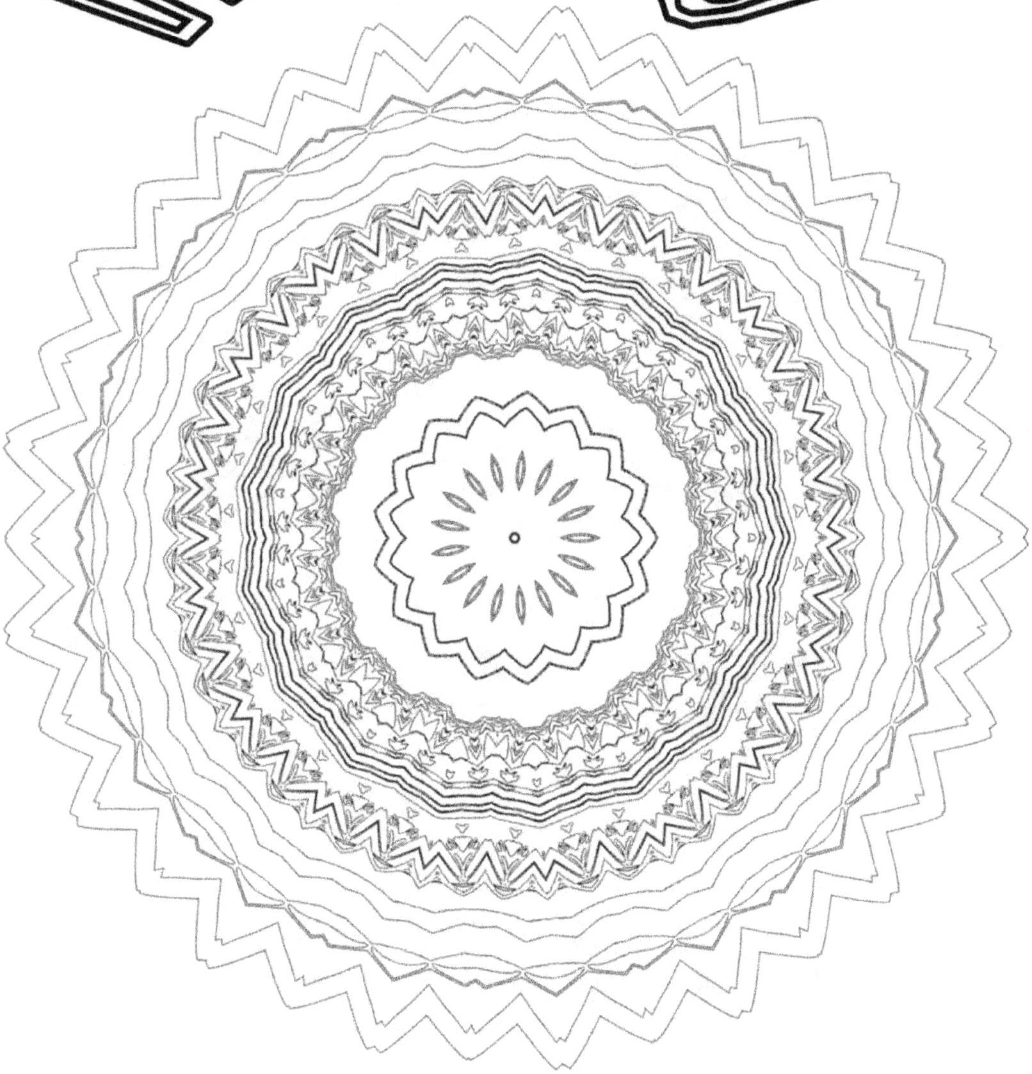

A Cup Of Love

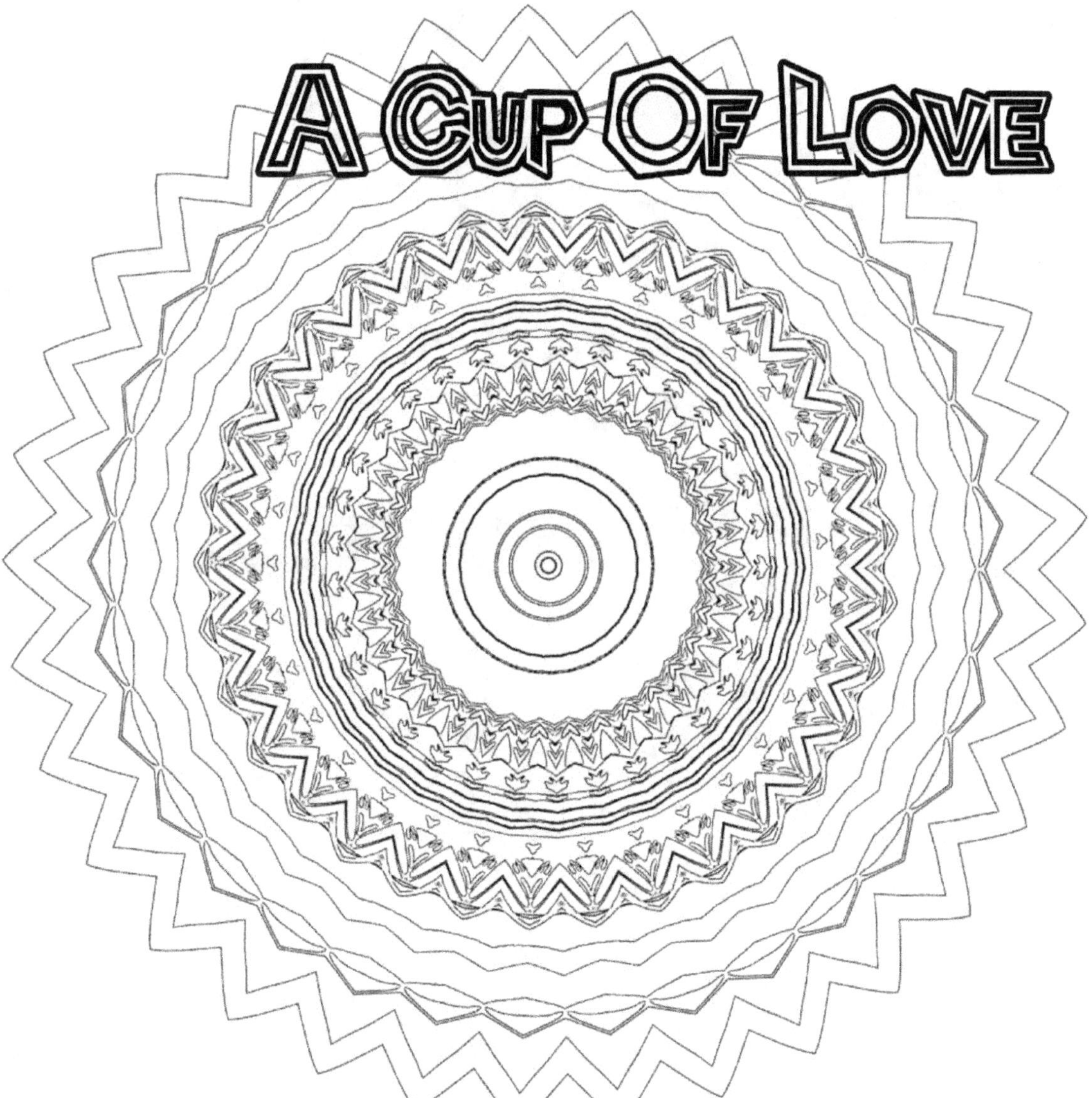

Love in the Mist

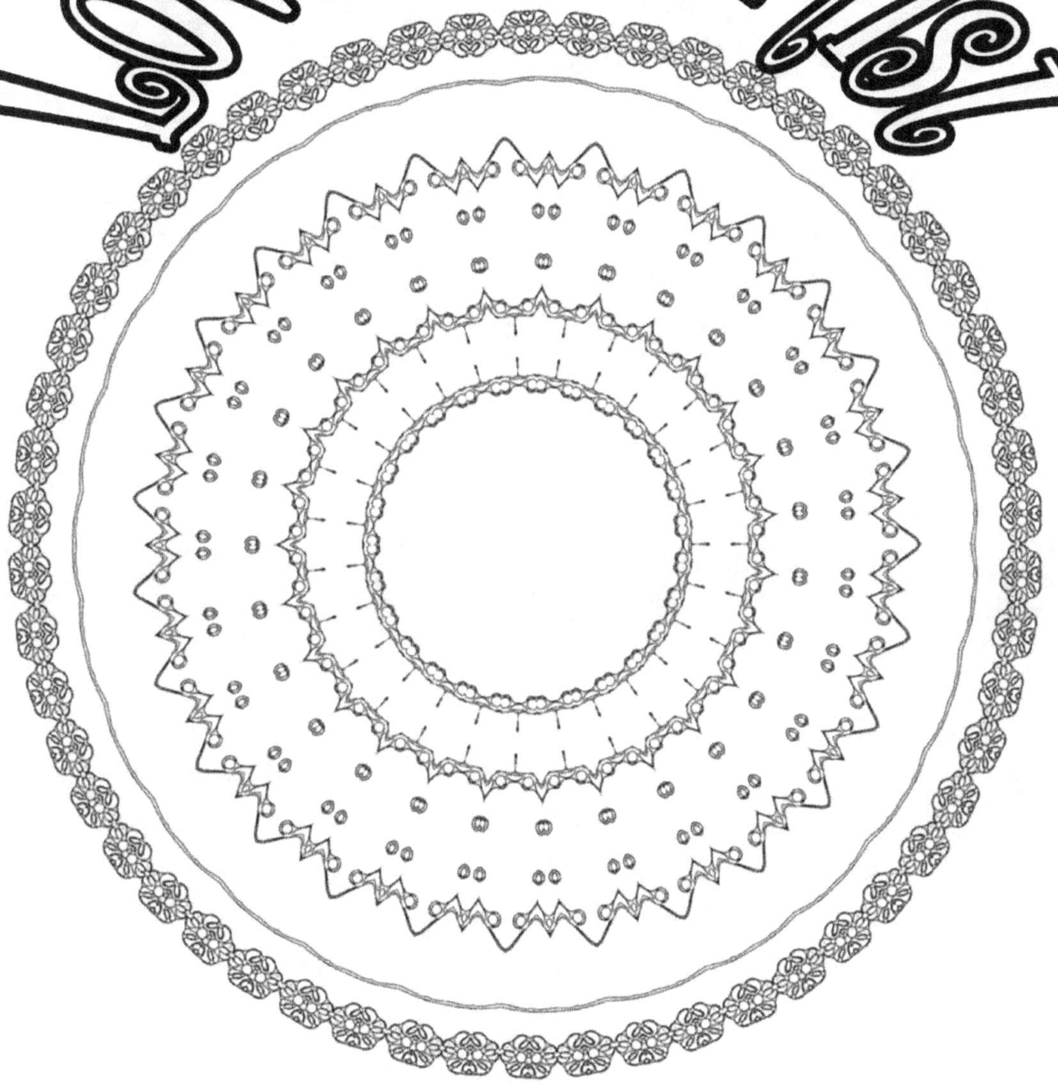

Love at the first site

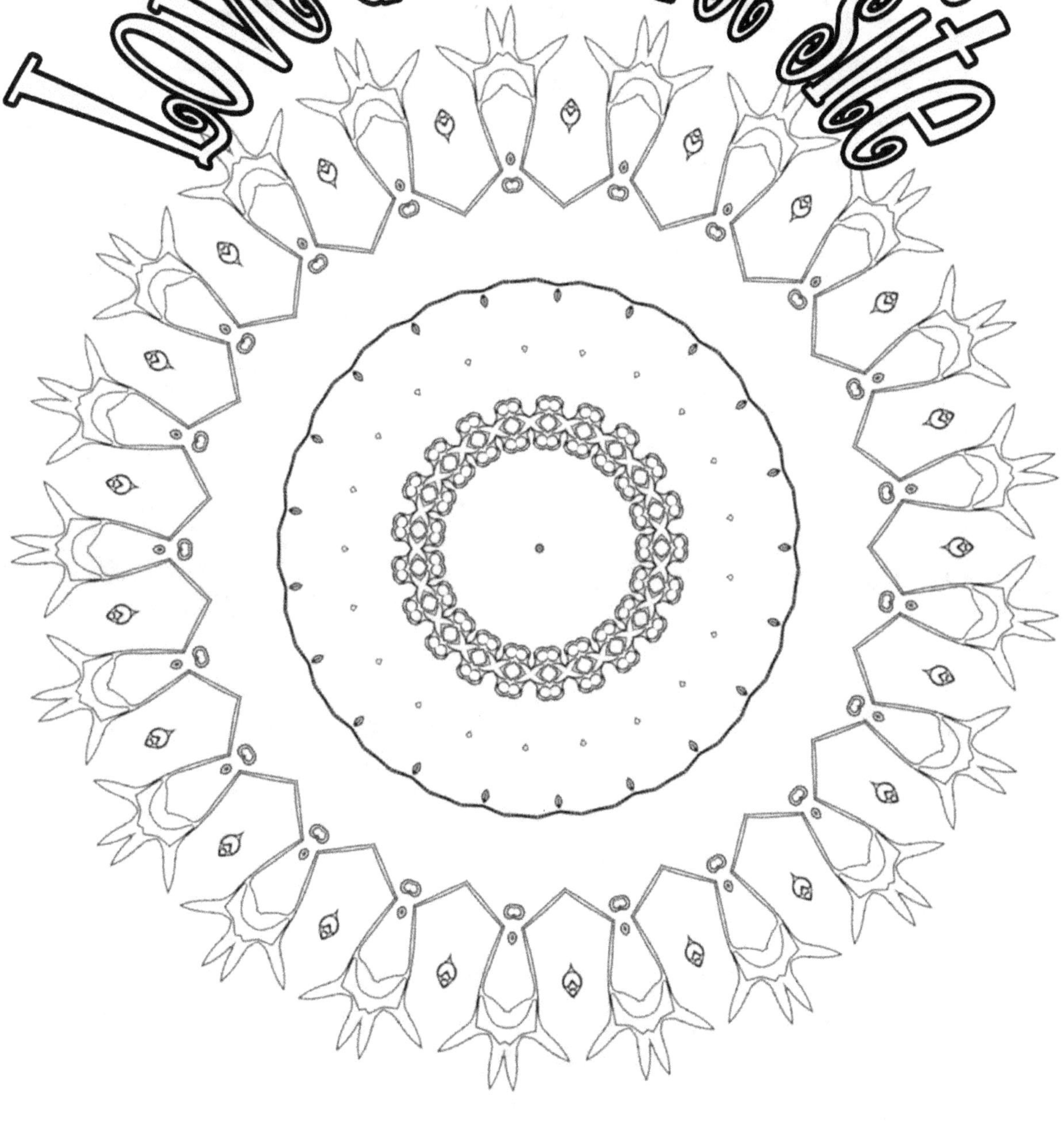

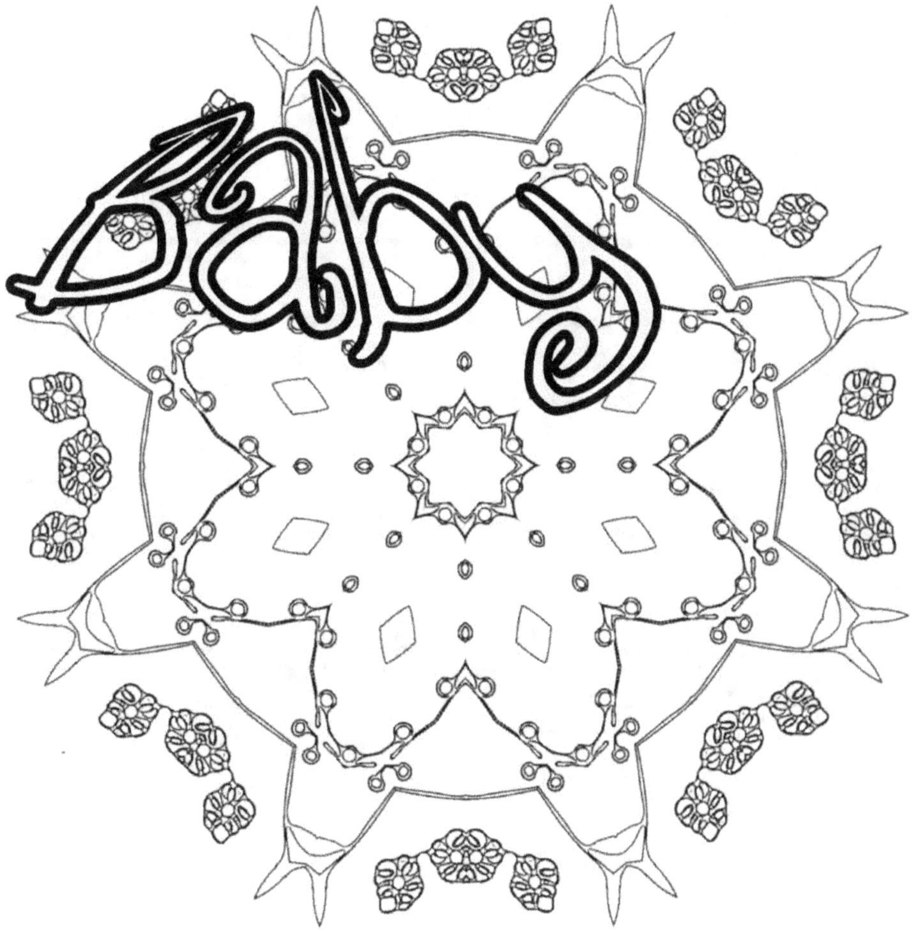
Baby

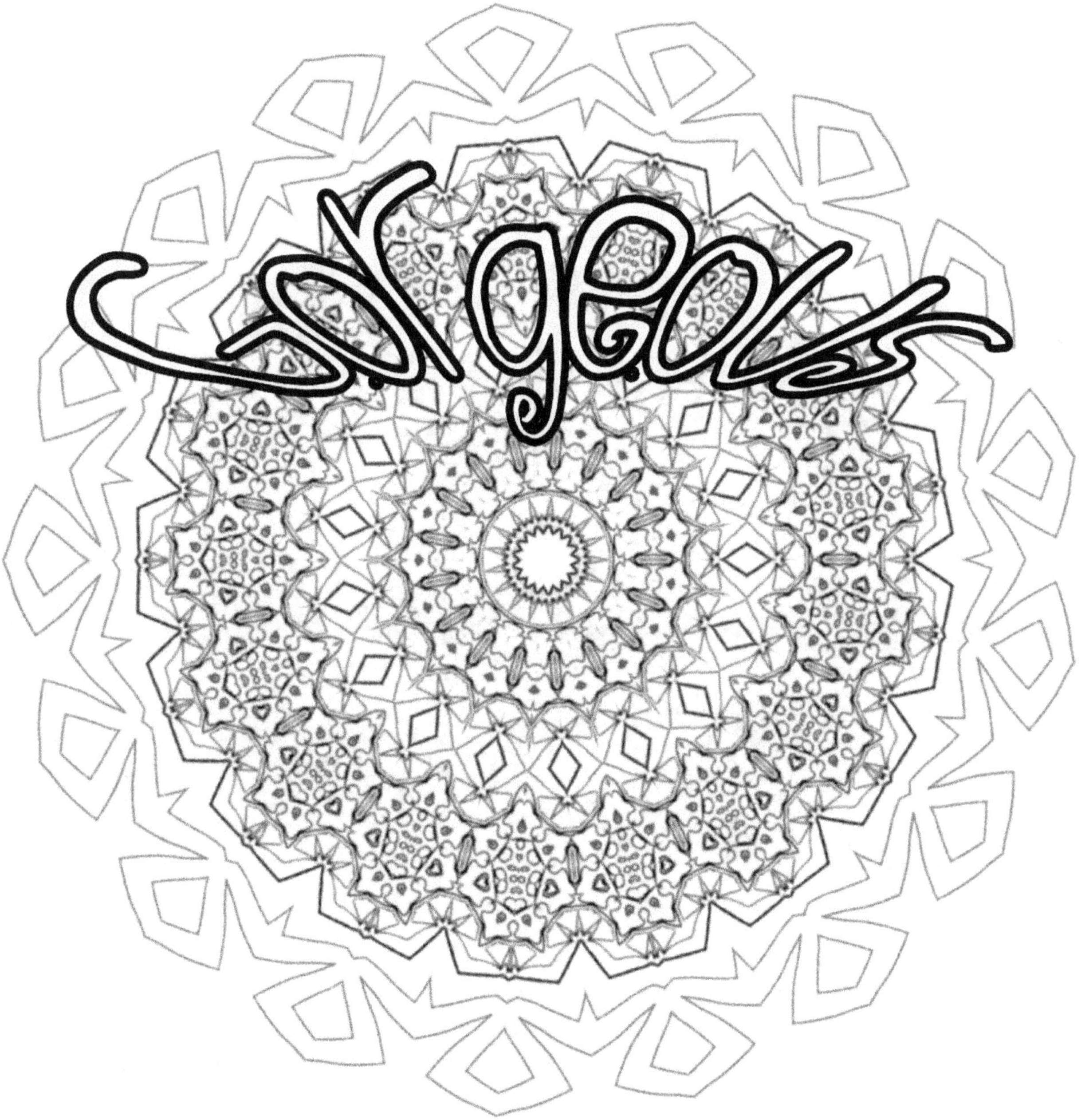

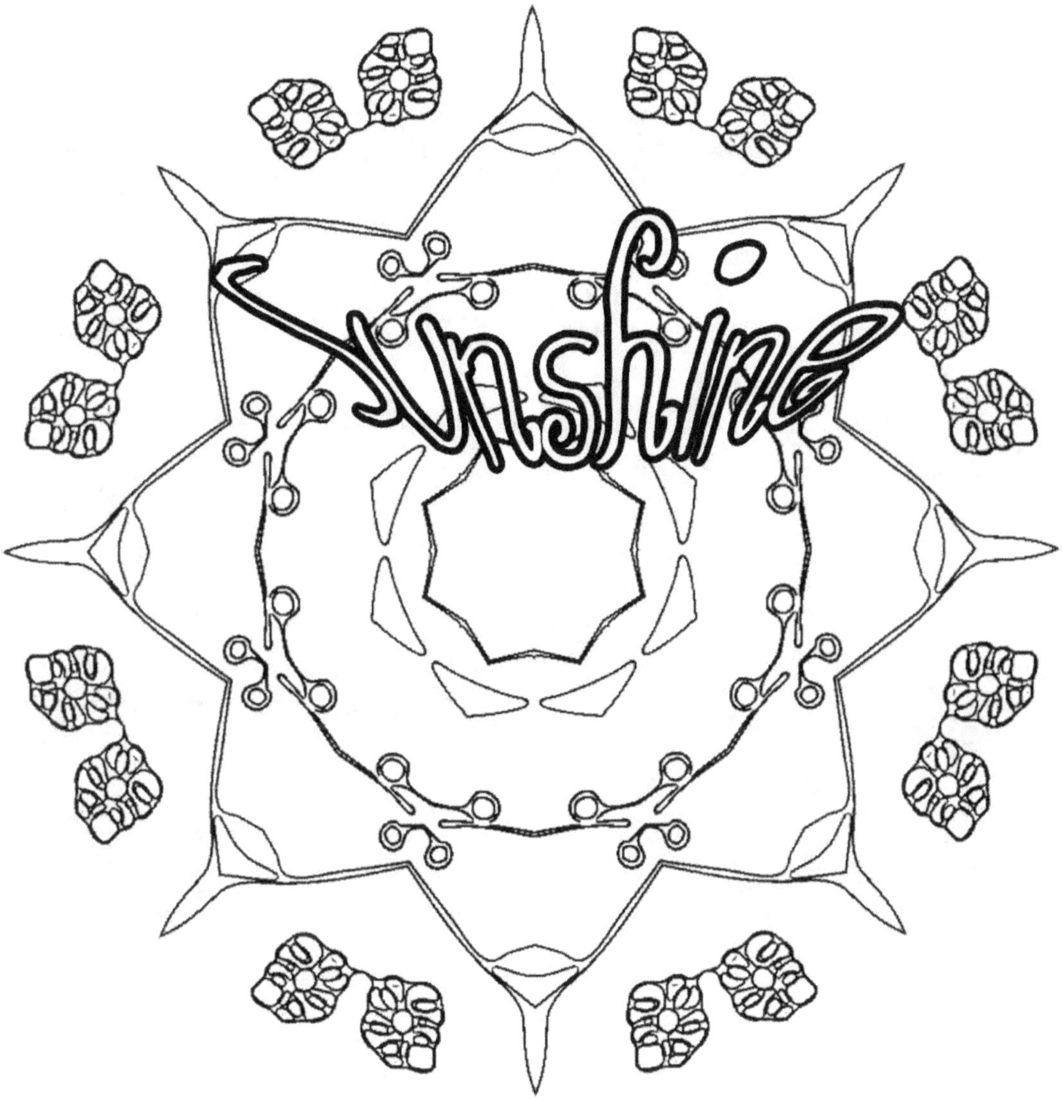
Sunshine

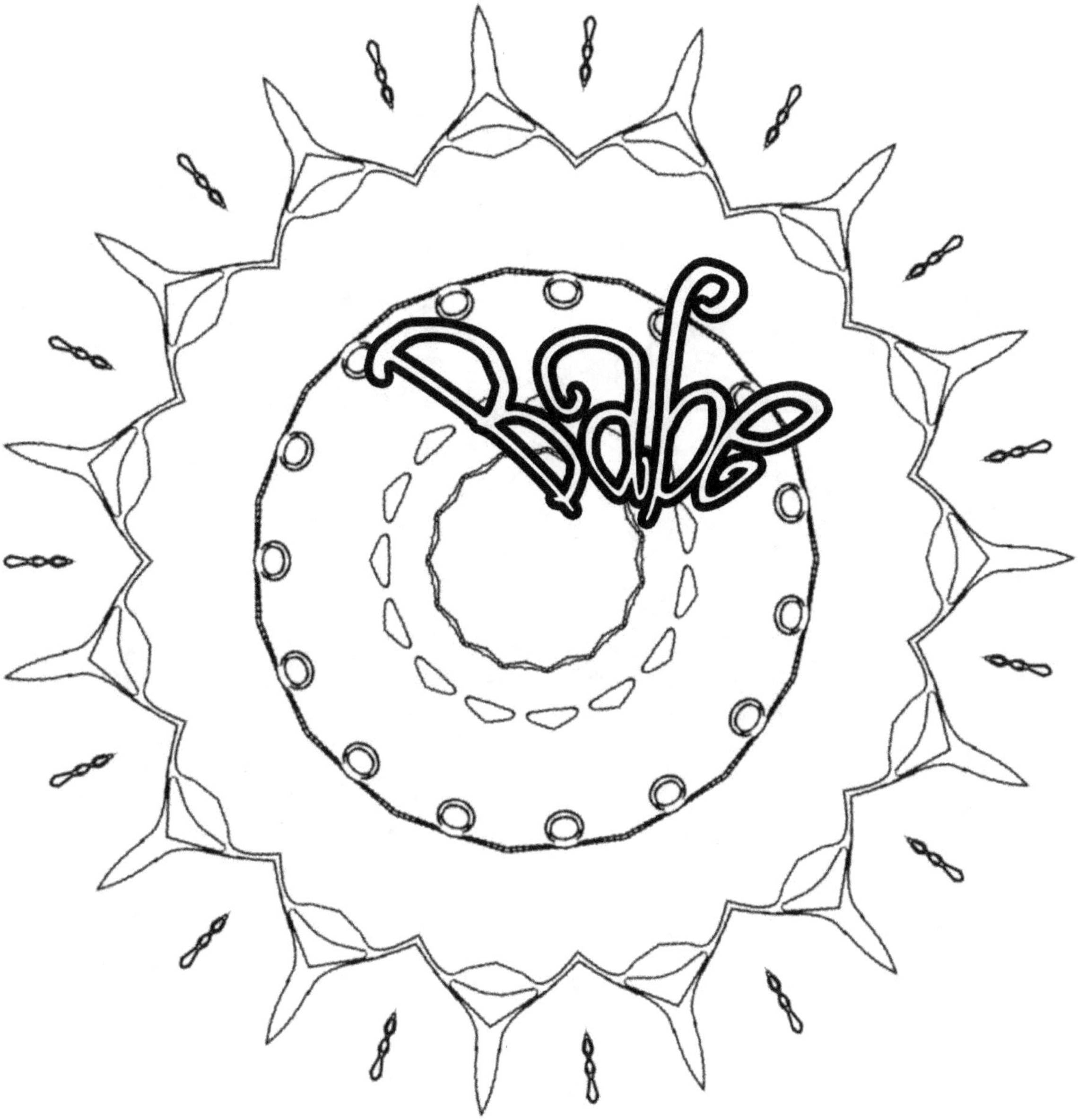
Babe

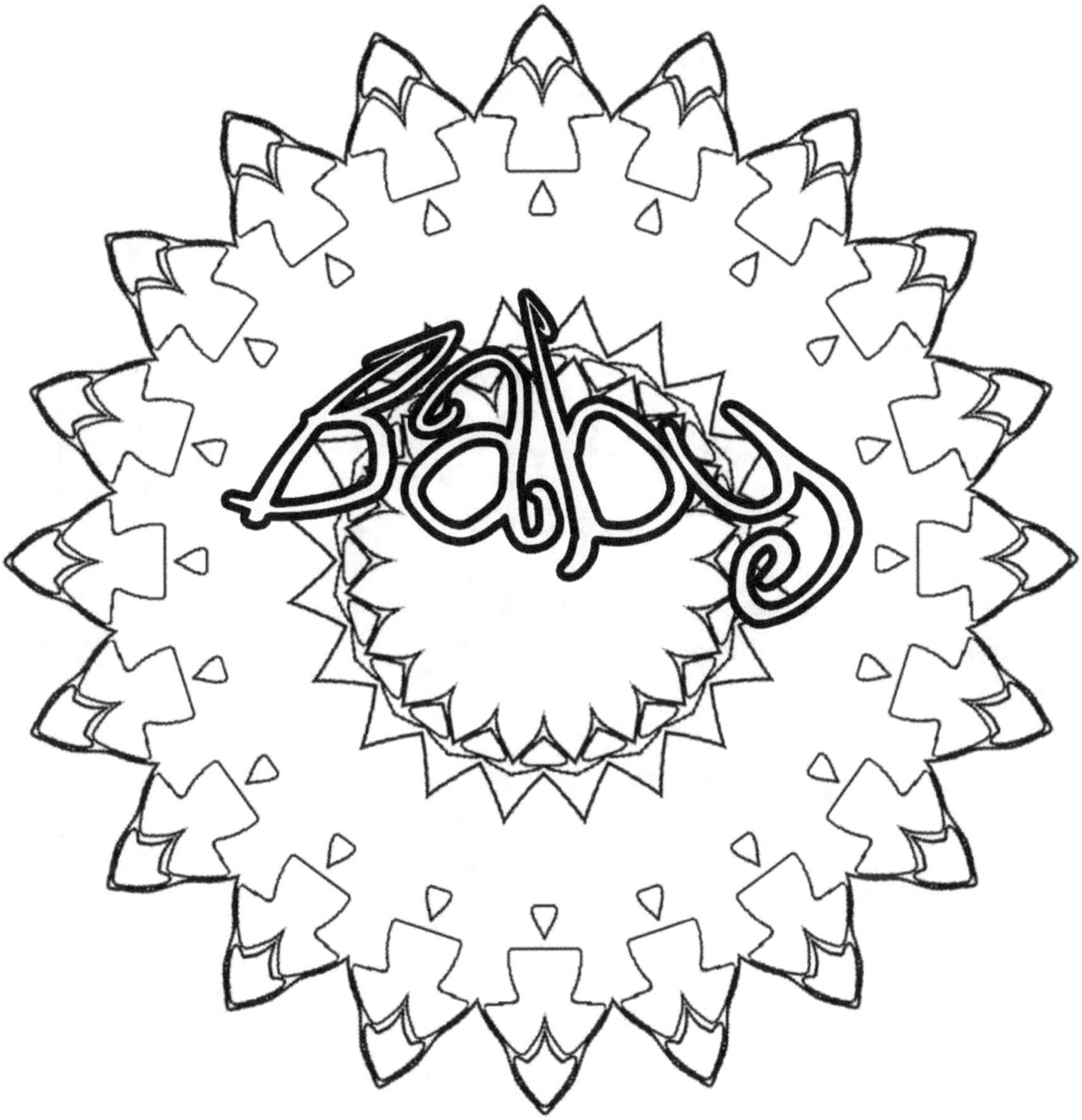
Baby

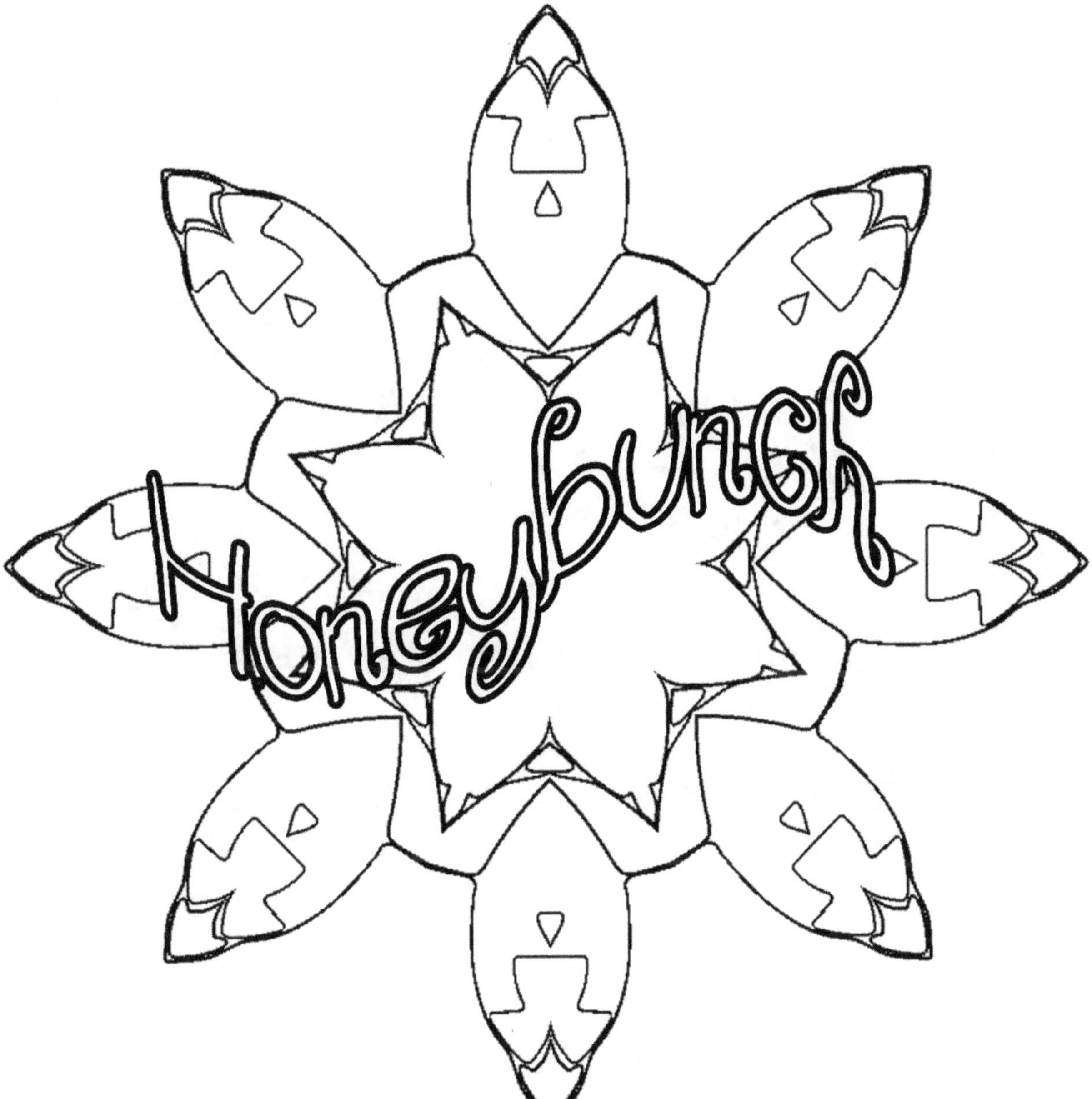
Honeybunch

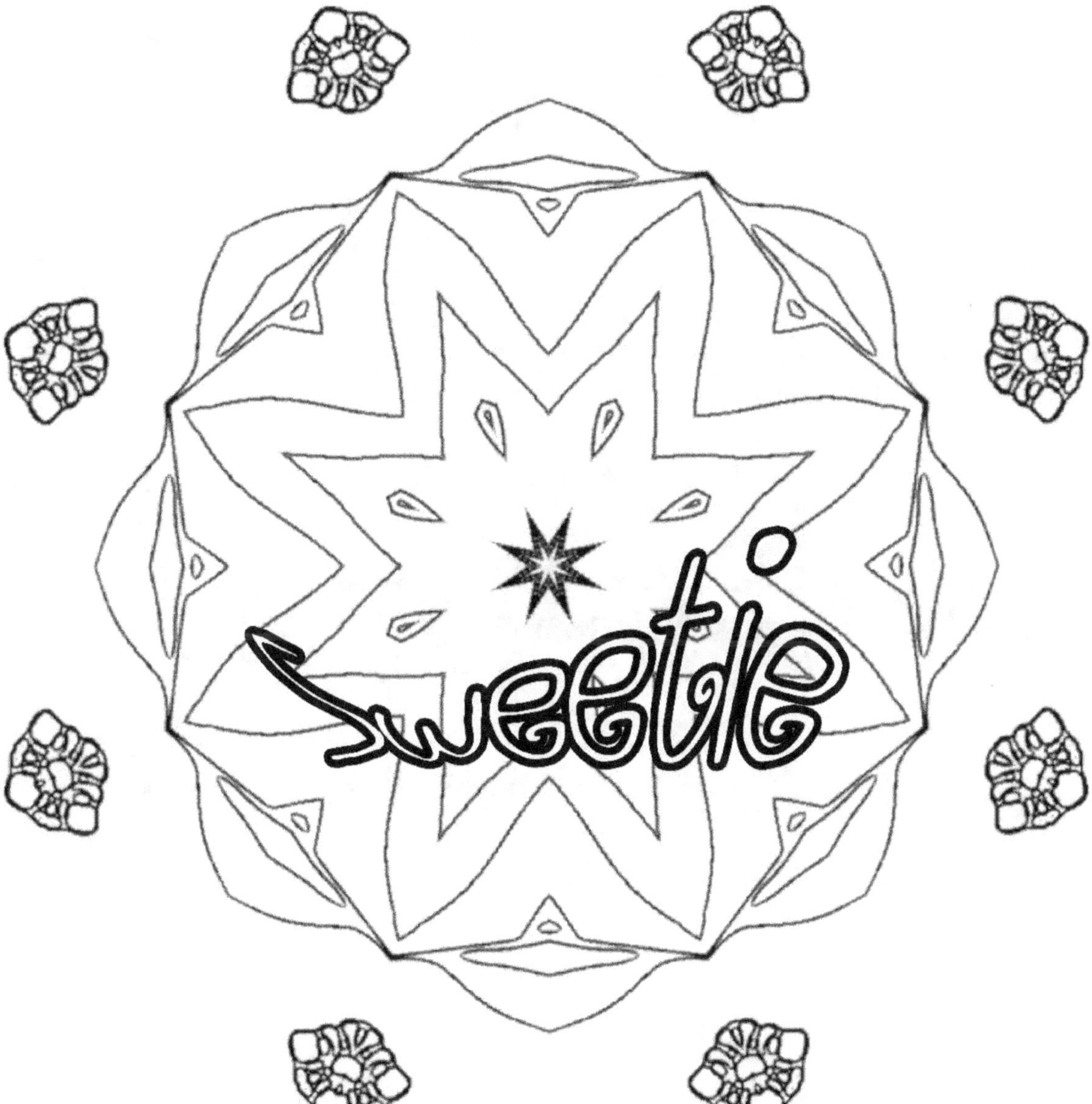
Sweetie

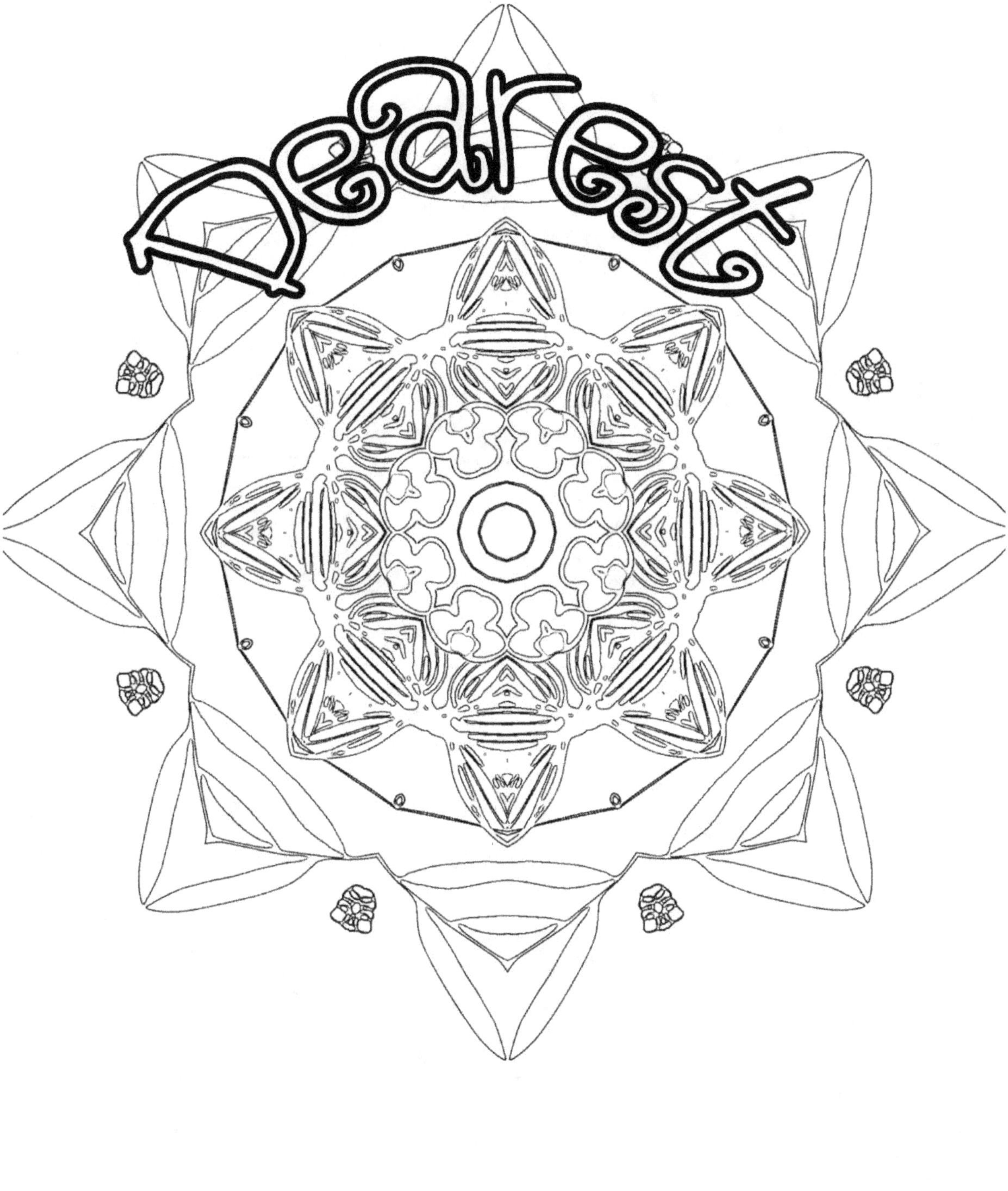
Dearest

www.ingramcontent.com/pod-product-compliance
Lightning Source LLC
Chambersburg PA
CBHW081749170526
45167CB00009B/3976
* 9 7 8 1 5 4 3 0 2 5 7 4 3 *